DIG AND DISCOVER
GEODES

by Nancy Dickmann

CAPSTONE PRESS
a capstone imprint

Published by Capstone Press, an imprint of Capstone
1710 Roe Crest Drive, North Mankato, Minnesota 56003
capstonepub.com

Library of Congress Cataloging-in-Publication Data is available on the Library of Congress website
ISBN: 9781666342567 (hardcover)
ISBN: 9781666342581 (paperback)
ISBN: 9781666342598 (ebook PDF)

Summary: Geodes look plain on the outside, but on the inside they're full of beautiful crystals. Uncover how these hollow rocks form and how to identify them.

All internet sites appearing in back matter were available and accurate when this book was sent to press.

DISCLAIMER:

This book provides information about various types of rocks and where and how to find them. Before entering any area in search of rocks, make sure that the area is open to the public or that you have secured permission from the property owner to go there. Also, take care not to damage any property, and do not remove any rocks from the area unless you have permission to do so.

Rock hunting in riverbeds, quarries, mines, and some of the other areas identified in this book can be inherently risky. You should not engage in any of these activities without parental supervision. Also, you should always wear proper safety equipment and know how to use any tools that you bring with you. You should not engage in any activity that is beyond your ability or skill or comfort level. Failure to follow these guidelines may result in damage to property or serious injury or death to you or others, and may also result in substantial civil or criminal liability.

The publisher and the author shall not be liable for any damages allegedly arising from the information in this book, and they specifically disclaim any liability from the use or application of any of the contents of this book.

Printed in the United States   5820

CONTENTS

Words in **bold** are in the glossary.

INTRODUCTION
A HIDDEN BEAUTY

Imagine you've been rock hunting in a desert or along a riverbed. You have a bucket of interesting stones. One is rough and lumpy. It looks pretty ordinary. But it feels a bit lighter than it should.

You're excited to get it home and see what's inside. Once it breaks open, you're amazed! Inside, it is hollow. The shell is coated with sparkling **crystals**. Your plain-looking rock wasn't so ordinary after all. It's a geode! These stones are a real treat for a **rock hound**.

Geodes are found in many locations around the world. People collect them as a hobby. You can collect them too!

Geodes can be fun additions to a rock collection!

CHAPTER 1
WHAT IS A GEODE?

Rocks are made of substances called **minerals**. Geodes are special kinds of hollow rocks. Many are plain on the outside. But their insides are lined with beautiful minerals. Their centers are always hollow. If a rock is solid all the way through, it isn't a geode. It's called a nodule instead. To tell if a rock is a geode, you have to split it open.

Most geodes have a rounded shape. The shell of a geode is hard and usually bumpy. Many geodes are about the size of a tennis ball. A few are much, much bigger. They're big enough to stand inside! These can have very large crystals.

The crystals inside a geode form inside the outer shell.

Some amethyst geodes are very large.

Inside a Geode

Geodes might look similar on the outside. But they are very different on the inside. It all depends on the type of mineral in them.

There are many mineral types. Some geodes have **quartz** crystals on the inside. Quartz can be different colors. Amethyst is a purple quartz. It is often found inside geodes. Agate is also common in geodes. The minerals in agate form bands of different colors. This gives it a striped appearance. A few rare geodes have **opals** inside. Some geodes are filled with tiny white crystals. They form lumps. The insides of these geodes look like piles of grapes!

Fantastic Find!

In 1999, mineral hunters were exploring an old silver mine in Spain. They found a geode so big it was like a cave. The Pulpí Geode is filled with huge crystals. Some of them are about 7 feet (2.1 meters) long! They are made of a see-through mineral called gypsum.

The Magic of Geodes

Geodes seem almost magical. They're like treasure chests made of stone! They are very popular at rock shows. Some of the most spectacular geodes are on display at museums. They are worth thousands of dollars.

People also put beautiful geodes in their homes. You can buy geodes at many stores. They are cut open to show the crystals inside. Sometimes they are cut into slices. They might even be dyed bright colors.

Some geodes sold in stores have been dyed to make them more colorful.

Geodes are not useful for building. Their main feature is their beauty! If you cut one in half, you get a pair of matching stones. Large geodes are often used as bookends. You can sand and polish the cut edges. This makes the geode look shiny and smooth.

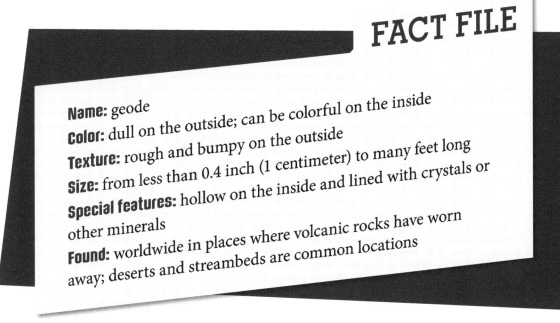

FACT FILE

Name: geode
Color: dull on the outside; can be colorful on the inside
Texture: rough and bumpy on the outside
Size: from less than 0.4 inch (1 centimeter) to many feet long
Special features: hollow on the inside and lined with crystals or other minerals
Found: worldwide in places where volcanic rocks have worn away; deserts and streambeds are common locations

CHAPTER 2
HOW GEODES FORM

The conditions have to be just right for a geode to form. When they are, many geodes can form in the same location. These amazing rocks form in two different ways.

When a volcano erupts, it spews out gas and **lava**. The lava is hot, melted rock. When the lava cools down, it turns hard. But some gas bubbles get trapped inside. They leave hollow places in the solid rock.

Other rocks form in layers. This type is **sedimentary rock**. Rivers carry dirt and little pieces of rock. These settle and form a layer. They are covered by more and more layers. The weight turns the layers into rock. Sometimes living things like tree roots are trapped inside. Over time, they will rot away. They leave hollow spaces behind.

As lava cools, bubbles inside it become hollow spaces in the resulting rock.

Fantastic Find!

In 2020, miners in Uruguay split open a rock. What was inside amazed them! A geode had formed inside the rock. It was filled with amethyst. And it was perfectly heart-shaped!

Filling the Gap

How do these hollow spaces get filled with crystals? It's all about water! Water seeps through the ground. Some of it enters the hollow spaces. The water carries minerals. They **dissolve** in the water.

Inside the space in the rock, the minerals make a hard outer layer of crystals. Over thousands or millions of years, more water enters. It leaves more crystals behind. They form layers. The water doesn't always have the same mix of minerals. A geode can have layers of different types.

Wind and water can wear away rock. Over time, the rock around the geode wears away. But the outer edge of the geode is harder. It looks rocky but is made of quartz. It doesn't wear away. The geode is now exposed. It will be easier for someone to find!

FACT

A geode fills up layer by layer. Sometimes the layers end up filling the entire cavity. The rock is no longer a geode. It's called a nodule instead. There is no hollow space inside.

HOW GEODES FORM

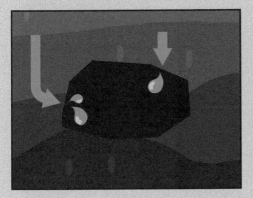

1. Mineral-rich water seeps into a hole in rock.

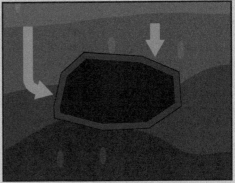

2. The minerals harden into a layer around the walls of the hole.

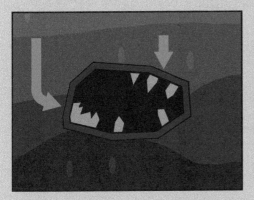

3. Mineral water continues to seep into the hole. Mineral crystals begin growing along the mineral layer.

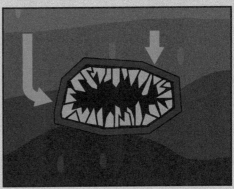

4. Crystals continue growing inward in the hole, partially filling it.

CHAPTER 3
GEODE TREASURE HUNT

Would you like to have your own geode? You can buy geode kits. They have rocks that you can crack open. But it's more fun to find your own!

You will find geodes only in places that have the right kinds of rock. The deserts of the American Southwest have many geodes. They formed in volcanic rock. Brazil has volcanic rock too. Large amethyst geodes are often found there.

FACT

Ametista do Sul is a town in Brazil. It is famous for amethysts and geodes. One of the town's churches has walls made of amethyst! The altar is a giant geode.

You must be patient when rock hunting. It might take a long time to find a geode.

There are also geodes in Iowa and other parts of the Midwest. These formed in sedimentary rock. They are often found in streambeds.

LAGUNA BEACH
STATE MARINE RESERVE

DO NOT!
REMOVE or DISTURB

Shells, Rocks, Plants or Marine Life

LBMC 18.29.030

Take Nothing; Leave Nothing

NO FISHING or SPEARFISHING

Always follow the rules when you are hunting for rocks.

Know the Rules

Rockhounding is allowed only in certain places. On private land, you need the owner's permission. On government land, you might need a permit. To protect nature, national and state parks may not allow rock collecting. Check the rules before you head out.

It's important to stay safe too. Always have an adult with you. Take a cell phone, water, snacks, a first aid kit, and sunscreen. Don't go into mines or caves. Stay away from cliff edges and bodies of water.

When hunting for geodes, bring a bucket or box to store your finds. Work gloves will help protect your hands. Sturdy boots will protect your feet.

FACT

There are geodes in the Mendip Hills of southern England. People there call them "potato stones"!

You can gather the rocks you think might be geodes in a basket to bring home.

Is It a Geode?

You can't tell for sure if a rock is a geode until you crack it open. But there are a few clues you can look for. Geodes are usually fairly small. Most are rounded or egg-shaped. They rarely have sharp edges. They aren't smooth, either. Most are lumpy, like cauliflower. They are often a bit light too. This is because of the hollow space inside.

If you think you've found a geode, ask yourself a few questions. Was it found in a desert or near a lake, stream, or river? Is it rounded? Is it bumpy? Does it feel a bit light? If you can answer "yes" to all of these questions, it might be a geode.

CHAPTER 4
WHAT'S INSIDE?

You've got a bag full of rocks that might be geodes. It's time to crack them open! Geodes have hard shells. Opening them up isn't easy. A **rock saw** will do the job. Rock shops often have these. They may saw rocks for a small fee. You can also open a geode at home. You'll need an adult to help.

The safest way is to put the geode inside a sock and then hit it with a geology hammer. Any sharp splinters of rock will stay in the sock. But you should still wear safety goggles, just in case.

You will get a neater cut with a hammer and chisel. This is a job for an adult. First, tap the chisel lightly around the outside of the rock. This is called scoring. After that, a few hard taps will split the geode open. It should split along the scored line.

Cracking open a geode with a hammer
may give you several pieces to enjoy.

FACT

Some geodes have **stalactites** inside! They hang
down like the stalactites in a cave. They are made of a
mineral called gem silica.

Sanding and Polishing

With luck, you'll have two equal pieces that fit together after you break a geode open. If you used a sock and a hammer, you might end up with several smaller pieces. You might like the way they look just as they are. But you can also polish the cut edges to make them shine.

Polishing a geode can help bring out some of its beautiful features.

Fantastic Find!

In 1897, workers were digging a well at a winery in Ohio. About 40 feet (12 m) down, they found a large cavern. And it was full of crystals! They had discovered a huge geode. Called the Crystal Cave, it is about 40 feet (12 m) long.

Clean the outside of your geode with warm, soapy water. Use an old toothbrush to clear away grit and dirt. Then it's time to sand the cut edges. Be ready for a long job! Start with rough sandpaper. When you can see a difference, switch to a finer sandpaper. Keep going finer until you get the look you want. Make sure to wear a mask so you don't breathe in rock dust.

CHAPTER 5
BUILDING YOUR COLLECTION

After it's polished, your geode is ready to display! It will be the star of your rock collection. You can't wait to show it to your friends.

Rock hounds often catalog their finds. They make a record for each rock. It has facts such as where the rock was found and what was inside. You can do this on a computer. You can also write it on a card. Then you can display it with the rock.

Geodes from the same area often have the same minerals inside. You can mark your finds on a map. Then you can compare your map with the finds of other rock hounds! They might know of other places where you can find geodes. These might have different minerals.

Building a rock collection can be a lot of fun.

SAMPLE CATALOG CARD

TYPE OF ROCK: geode

WHEN FOUND: June 2, 2022

WHERE FOUND: on the banks of Cutter Stream

COLOR: tan on the outside, white calcite crystals on the inside

TEXTURE: slightly bumpy

SHAPE: round

SIZE: 6 cm across

NOTES: I had it cut open at the rock shop.

There are many ways to display your collection!

Making a Display

How do you want to display your geode? If it's really pretty, you might put it on a shelf. You can also keep it with the rest of your rock collection. Some people buy cases to display their rocks.

You can make your own case from a cardboard box. Use strips of cardboard to divide it into sections. Make pads from cotton balls to protect the rocks. Add a label for each one, and your collection is ready to show off! You could show it to your family, friends, and classmates.

Clubs

Once you have some experience rockhounding, why not join a club? You'll meet other rock hounds. They might have tips on where to find more geodes. The club might even arrange rock hunting trips. You never know what you'll find next!

Joining a club can help increase your chances of finding a geode.

GLOSSARY

crystal (KRI-stul)—a solid substance having a regular pattern, often with many flat surfaces

dissolve (di-ZOLV)—to mix completely into a liquid

lava (LAH-vuh)—the hot, liquid rock that pours out of a volcano when it erupts

mineral (MIN-ur-uhl)—a substance found in nature that is not made by a plant or animal

opal (OH-puhl)—a gemstone known for its shimmering rainbow colors

quartz (KWORTS)—a mineral made from silica that forms crystals with flat faces

rock hound (ROK HAUND)—someone who looks for and collects rocks as a hobby

rock saw (ROK SAW)—an electric saw with a spinning blade that is powerful enough to cut through rock

sedimentary rock (sed-uh-MEN-tur-ee RAHK)—rock that formed from layers of material like sand and dirt that were laid down and pressed together

stalactite (stuh-LAK-tite)—an icicle-like structure made from minerals and that hangs from the roof of a cave

ultraviolet light (uhl-truh-VYE-uh-lit LITE)—a type of light that humans can't see directly but which makes certain substances glow

READ MORE

Lewis, Gary. *My Awesome Field Guide to Rocks & Minerals: Track and Identify Your Treasures.* Emeryville, CA: Rockridge Press, 2019.

Potenza, Alessandra. *All About Rocks: Discovering the World Beneath Your Feet.* New York: Children's Press, 2021.

Swanson, Jennifer. *Rock, Fossil, and Shell Hunting.* New York: Odd Dot, 2021.

INTERNET SITES

American Museum of Natural History: Start a Rock Collection amnh.org/explore/ology/earth/start-a-rock-collection2

Gem Kids: The Story of a Gem: What Are Minerals? gemkids.gia.edu/gem-story?chapter=1

Wonderopolis: What Is a Geode? wonderopolis.org/wonder/what-is-a-geode

INDEX

ABOUT THE AUTHOR

Nancy Dickmann grew up reading encyclopedias for fun, and after many years working in children's publishing, she now has her dream job as a full-time author. She has had over 200 titles published so far, mainly on science topics, and finds that the best part of the job is researching and learning new things. One highlight was getting to interview a real astronaut to find out about using the toilet in space!

Editorial Credits
Editor: Marie Pearson; Designer: Joshua Olson; Production Specialists: Joshua Olson and Polly Fisher